From Seed to Crop

Level 4 – Blue

Helpful Hints for Reading at Home

The graphemes (written letters) and phonemes (units of sound) used throughout this series are aligned with Letters and Sounds. This offers a consistent approach to learning whether reading at home or in the classroom.

THIS PHASE OF LEARNING BUILDS ON PHONEMES FROM THE PREVIOUS PHASE. HERE IS THE LIST OF PHONEMES FROM THE PREVIOUS PHASE. AN EXAMPLE OF THE PRONUNCIATION CAN BE FOUND IN BRACKETS.

Phase 3			
j (jug)	v (van)	w (wet)	x (fox)
y (yellow)	z (zoo)	zz (buzz)	qu (quick)
ch (chip)	sh (shop)	th (thin/then)	ng (ring)
ai (rain)	ee (feet)	igh (night)	oa (boat)
oo (boot/look)	ar (farm)	or (for)	ur (hurt)
ow (cow)	oi (coin)	ear (dear)	air (fair)
ure (sure)	er (corner)		

HERE ARE SOME WORDS WHICH YOUR CHILD MAY FIND TRICKY.

Phase 3 Tricky Words			
he	you	she	they
we	all	me	are
be	my	was	her

Phase 4 Tricky Words			
said	were	have	there
like	little	so	one
do	when	some	out
come	what		

TOP TIPS FOR HELPING YOUR CHILD TO READ:

- Allow children time to break down unfamiliar words into units of sound and then encourage children to string these sounds together to create the word.

- Encourage your child to point out any focus phonics when they are used.

- Read through the book more than once to grow confidence.

- Ask simple questions about the text to assess understanding.

- Encourage children to use illustrations as prompts.

PHASE 4 /ow/ /oi/

This book focuses on the phonemes /ow/ and /oi/ and is a blue level 4 book band.

How many words can you list with o**i** in?

This is a seed. We can get a crop from the seed.

Seed

How will the crop look when it is big?

The seed can go down in the soil.

Seeds can go in a pot too. Soil must be in the pot.

Soon, the crop will join the top of the soil. It will go up and up.

The crop needs liquid to get big.
The soil must be moist.

The crop needs light from the Sun to get big.

The crop gets food from the Sun.

We can pick it off the crop when it is red.

Now it is red. We can pick it off!

It went from green to red. Now it is big. Wow!

Now we have a lot of food. What can we do with it?

©2022 **BookLife Publishing Ltd.**
King's Lynn, Norfolk PE30 4LS

ISBN 978-1-80155-102-1

All rights reserved. Printed in Poland.
A catalogue record for this book is available from the British Library.

From Seed to Crop
Written by Shalini Vallepur
Designed by Gareth Liddington

An Introduction to BookLife Readers...

Our Readers have been specifically created in line with the London Institute of Education's approach to book banding and are phonetically decodable and ordered to support each phase of Letters and Sounds.

Each book has been created to provide the best possible reading and learning experience. Our aim is to share our love of books with children, providing both emerging readers and prolific page-turners with beautiful books that are guaranteed to provoke interest and learning, regardless of ability.

BOOK BAND GRADED using the Institute of Education's approach to levelling.

PHONETICALLY DECODABLE supporting each phase of Letters and Sounds.

EXERCISES AND QUESTIONS to offer reinforcement and to ascertain comprehension.

CLEAR DESIGN to inspire and provoke engagement, providing the reader with clear visual representations of each non-fiction topic.

AUTHOR INSIGHT:
SHALINI VALLEPUR

Passionate about books from a very young age, Shalini Vallepur received the award of Norfolk County Scholar for her outstanding grades. Later on she read English at the University of Leicester, where she stayed to complete her Modern Literature MA. Whilst at university, Shalini volunteered as a Storyteller to help children learn to read, which gave her experience and expertise in the way children pick up and retain information. She used her knowledge and her background and implemented them in the 32 books that she has written for BookLife Publishing. Shalini's writing easily takes us to different worlds, and the serenity and quality of her words are sure to captivate any child who picks up her books.

PHASE 4 /ow/ /oi/

This book focuses on the phonemes /ow/ and /oi/ and is a blue level 4 book band.

Image Credits Images are courtesy of Shutterstock.com. With thanks to Getty Images, Thinkstock Photo and iStockphoto. Cover – Ian 2010, Vasenina Daria, melaics, irin-k, VIEW17. 3 – Phant, Italian Food Production, Henning Marquardt, domnitsky, Elena Zajchikova. 4&5 – Yellow Cat, Imfoto, somkanae sawatdinak, Sergiy Kuzmin. 6&7 – amenic181, Ramil gibadullin. 8&9 – kram–9, Oleg Mikhaylov. 10&11 – fotohunter. 12&13 – Dzha33, Tatiana Bobkova. 14&15 – stevemart, fizkes.